SUNDAY FUNNIES

Jay Sidebotham

MOREHOUSE PUBLISHING

HARRISBURG • PENNSYLVANIA

Morehouse Publishing, P.O. Box 1321, Harrisburg, PA 17105
Morehouse Publishing, 445 Fifth Avenue, New York, NY 10016
Morehouse Publishing is an imprint of Church Publishing Incorporated.

Cover art: Jay Sidebotham

Library of Congress Cataloging-in-Publication Data

Sidebotham, Jay.
  Sunday funnies / Jay Sidebotham.
     p. cm.
  ISBN-13: 978-0-8192-2205-3 (pbk.)
  1. Church—Caricatures and cartoons. I. Title.
  BV600.3.S53 2006
  741.5'6973—dc22
                                    2006005489

Printed in the United States of America

06 07 08 09   10 9 8 7 6 5 4 3 2 1

Dedicated to

Frances, John Reid, and Helen,
who always make me smile.

CONTENTS

FOREWORD

E. B. WHITE ONCE OBSERVED that "humor can be dissected, as a frog can, but the thing dies in the process and the innards are discouraging to any but the pure scientific mind."

No one need analyze Jay Sidebotham's cartoons. They are simply and wonderfully enjoyable. Period. I wouldn't blame you for turning to them right now.

If you stay here for a moment, you'll find a few thoughts about the persistence of humor and hope in one of the true bastions of seriousness, the Church. I offer them in tribute to Jay's sense of humor and in thanksgiving for God's gift of humor to us all.

If you think only the Church is humor-challenged, consider the case of a semester-long graduate seminar offered some years ago at the august University of Chicago. The premise of the course, called "The Theory of Comedy" and taught by a dour neo-Aristolelian, was that "comedy was to be understood as an eternal structural form for literature, not a mere occasion for jokes." In fact, jokes were never told. We are reliably informed by a survivor of the course, "we had to devise our own amusements."

Thank God, it has always been so. In prisoner-of-war camps, deadly offices, stressed-out families, emergency rooms, operating rooms, and, of course, terminally serious churches, people have to devise their own funnies. It's a matter of survival.

But good as our survival instincts are, the joke is how easily we lose our humor. There are now several businesses that guarantee that deadly business places can come alive by using humor. They promise to transform unhappy drones into creative and resilient workers. They offer workshops, consultants, teleconferences, and workbooks—and a bill for services rendered. Does the specimen laugh, or die?

As one who has been privileged to work with Jay in ministry, I know a different kind of approach. I also know that the pleasure of being one of the dissected. It doesn't hurt. It heals. All good humor heals when it is based on love.

Jay's humor is not only loving, it is knowing. One needs to know the church and still love it to be a healer with humor.

He knows as so many of us do that the Church is often a temple of seriousness. As such, it's caught in a classic double-bind. We come to church for serious reasons: the worship of the awesome Creator, the confession of our own mistakes and foibles, the healing of a broken world. Our methods are serious, too. We preach discipline. We urge reflection.

But that is just what gets us in trouble. We forget the crucial distinction between taking our work seriously and ourselves lightly. The result is the rueful picture we sometimes present: people who aren't having very much fun.

Settle down with a daily dose of Jay's loving look at us, and that may begin to change. Laugh. Give this book to others, and you may unleash change right where it's needed most. A little healing for the potential healers of the world is a good thing.

It will be obvious that the context for Jay's fun is the local Christian congregation. There are over 300,000 of these vital communities in America. Society needs these spiritual forces as much as their members do.

Christian is defined in this context simply as the people and places who continue the work Jesus once did on earth. Again—see "dissecting" above—we can't test for the source of a cartoonist's gift. I choose to think it is one part gift of God and one part raw talent. But surely the talent is informed by the master humorist, Jesus.

Yes. Maybe you had to be there, but those who've really lived with the Gospels, for instance, and not just studied them at arm's length can appreciate how much stand-up there was in Jesus' teaching.

While others were debating religious law, he had the crowds laughing at the "sawdust speck in your neighbor's eye but not the log in your own eye." He kept the people on his side when he joked that the serious but clueless theologians could "strain out a gnat but swallow a camel," or skewered the fat cats as he famously joked that "it is easer for a camel to go through the eye of a needle" than for the rich to enter the Kingdom.

There are many places in Jesus' stories and the stories about him where we can laugh or hear the laughing of the original hearers. But it takes some softening up (or study, if you will) to get to those places.

In the pages that follow, you'll find yourself in the hands of one who softens souls to enjoy the church and enjoy its work.

G. K. Chesterton wrote that he was all in favor of laughing. "Laughing has something in common with the ancient words of faith and inspiration; it unfreezes pride and unwinds secrecy; it makes us forget ourselves in the presence of something greater than ourselves."

The biblical interpreter Conrad Hyers would have us remember that "humor is not the opposite of seriousness. Humor is the opposite of despair."

If Jay's cartoons, gentle dissections of the church, help you laugh at and with the church, then there is hope.

God in heaven knows we need that now more than ever.

William Tully
Rector, St. Bartholomew's Church
New York

INTRODUCTION

FROM ITS FIRST DAYS, the church has provided lots of comic material. For example, Jesus describes Peter as the rock on which the church would be built. What kind of rock was he? And can't you see Jesus smiling his way through the image of a camel going through the eye of a needle, comparing that excruciating exercise to a rich man parting with his possessions? Jesus got in trouble with authorities, partly because he was having too good a time. Jesus' adversaries didn't like John the Baptist because John was way too serious. They didn't like Jesus because he was always wining and dining with tax collectors and sinners (John 10:10).

Over the years, the church has come perilously close to losing its ability to laugh at itself, giving into a seriousness that is borderline terminal. But despite these tendencies, the church continues to provide opportunities for laughter. When you consider how the church doesn't always live up to what it's called to do and to be, you could laugh or you could cry.

As a student at Union Seminary in New York, contending with my short attention span and dim intelligence in comparison to the brighter lights of some of my colleagues, I found that appropriation of the heady theological material was eased as I rendered cartoons in the margins of my lecture notes. I soon found that my esteemed colleagues would look over my shoulder to see how I had made light of these enlightening presentations. I learned then that a picture, especially a funny picture, can truly be worth a thousand words. Since then, as a priest in the Episcopal Church, I've found that a cartoon or a light drawing will open doors that no amount of exegesis will crack.

This book is intended to make you smile. Not to laugh at the church, but to laugh with it. The book is designed to help us realize that in all of our foibles, God is still with us, accepting us with our shortcomings, in their great number and variety. For me, that is the heart of the gospel. That is grace. Finally, the book is meant to relieve the anxiety that often surfaces in the church, anxiety that keeps us from seeing how God is present among us. Enjoy this book. Let it remind you of the danger of taking life too seriously. And let it be a reminder that God is at work in us and through us and in spite of us.

The Rev. Jay Sidebotham

CHAPTER 1

The Bible Tells Me So—Sort Of
Biblical Moments That Didn't Make the Editor's Cut

THE BIBLE, assembled over many centuries, is filled with stories about ordinary people. And as we all know, people are funny. Imagine some of the conversations that went on behind the scenes. Imagine supporting actors and actresses whose minor roles never made it into the scriptural canon of the church. Let your imagination take you into what Karl Barth called the "strange world of the Bible." And celebrate the gift of our sacred text that in all kinds of ways reminds us of the amazing fact that we, with all our humorous foibles, are invited into relationship with the God of creation.

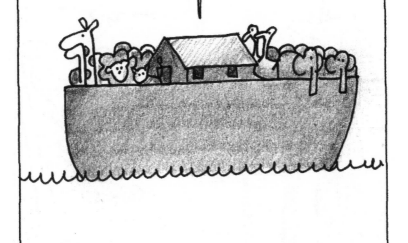

One of St. Paul's letters
gets delivered.

Overheard at Bible Study

CHAPTER 2

A Little Child Shall Lead Them
The Wit and Wisdom of the Youngest among Us

JESUS TIRED OF the serious religionists of his day, those who pressed in on him with all kinds of technical questions about how the law applied. One day, he heard kids making noise on the edge of the crowd. Adults tried to keep the children quiet, but Jesus had another idea. He stopped the proceedings and said (in so many words): "Bring those children front and center. They know something about the kingdom of heaven that you adults have totally missed." Children continue to show us the way, even as adults try to silence them in church, and push them to the edges in society. The following cartoons, some of which illustrate actual children's prayers and letters to God, show how that is true.

Dear God. My grandfather says you were around when he was a little boy. How far back do you go?
NEWS

CHAPTER 3

Making It through the Church Year
The Joys and Challenges of Church,
52 Sundays of the Year

EVERY YEAR, as we move through the seasons of the year and observe holy days, we tell the story of our faith over and over again. As we do, we live into the truth that we don't need to be instructed in the faith as much as we need to be reminded of it. These cartoons carry us through the year, with a particular eye on the intersection of the sacred and secular calendars. Enjoy them, remembering that time flies when you're having fun.

Pastor, we love your church. But you don't seem to do much about observing the season of Lent.
Oh, it's such a downer. We think Lent should be an acronym: Let's end negative thinking.

CHAPTER 4

Overheard at Church
Glimpses of Congregational Life

I ONCE PRESIDED AT a Bible study in which we studied the gospel of Matthew. In the middle of the study, a gentleman stood and said in response to the text before us: "Where two or three are gathered together . . . [long silence] . . . strange things happen." We can either laugh or cry at community life. The following cartoons offer varied snapshots of life in the church, highlighting any number of idiosyncrasies that surface in congregations. They remind us that as people of faith, we are not perfect, just forgiven. So we give thanks for community of life. With all its imperfections, it is a gift.

Your sermon spoke to me from the very start. When you said 'Please be seated', I thought about how I needed to slow down and I didn't need to hear another word.
Glad I spent so much time preparing.

CHAPTER 5

Modern Times
The Lighter Side of Church and Change

IN EACH GENERATION, the church must examine what it is called to do and to be. This means that the church is always a work in progress. As traditions get passed on from generation to generation, the church always stands in need of reform. We must "grow or go." For centuries, those who have sought to reform the church have run into the dreaded words, "We've never done it that way." Take these cartoons as an occasion to consider the ways the church carries out its mission in modern times. Celebrate the creativity of the human spirit that finds new ways to be the church. And think about what new ways you can discover to bring the faith to life these days.